Words of Love and Life:
An Emotional Journey

By J'Wan Yvette

© 2007 J'Wan Yvette
Published by Lulu Publishing
Lulu ID: 721018

ISBN: 978-0-6151-8879-9

Table of Contents:

V. Romantic Love, Fantasy, and Crushes

1. Complete
2. My Love
3. Love Turns to Hate
4. Unbreakable
5. Why?
6. I Care For You
7. Worlds Apart
8. Rhyme or Reason
9. Close To You
10. Pleasure Meets Pain
11. The Chase
12. You May Not Have My Number
13. Beautiful
14. Without You
15. Something beautiful Remains
16. With All My Heart
17. I Wish
18. Why (original)
19. Invisible
20. Broken
21. What's Missing
22. Damaged
23. What If
24. He Is My Drug
25. Taking It Back
26. How Ironic
27. Puppet
28. Puppet – Part 2
29. I Hate You
30. Empty
31. Puppet – Part 3
32. More Than a Crush
33. If These Walls Could Talk
34. Man of My Dreams
35. My Everything
36. My Secret Wish
37. If Only You Knew
38. I'm Sorry
39. I'm Yours

Based On a True Story

I started writing poetry when I was about 5 years old. When I was in high school, I wrote "Abstract Truth". I was feeling disappointed in a lot of what I saw around me. I was raised to believe in fairness and truth but all around me I saw violence, lies, unfairness and inequality. It hurt me to see girls willing to settle for being objectified as if that's all they deserved. I didn't want to become a part of the madness. So I wrote about it, and expressed my protest in words.

"A Mile in My Shoes" was born out of frustration after dealing with depression. It starts out dark, but the true message is in the last verse. And finally "Innocence Lost... A Life Redeemed" is based on the life of someone who became very close to me. I only knew A.J. for a little over a year before she tragically lost her life to a bullet. But she was like family to me, and I miss her greatly.

Abstract Truth

She lives in a world all her own. It's filled with love and acceptance, yet she's filled with fear and rage. Why? She can't explain.

In her world her sisters love her; she's never without a friend. In her world, a man's love is only a heartbeat away. Her spirit is free here. As she looks through the window into their world, she sees confusion. No love, just sex. No caring; just a battle for power. No brotherhood/sisterhood, just greed. It's a cruel world. She feels no acceptance there, no love. She feels only cold… sometimes abused. She cannot survive.

She returns to her world where she does not have to face the cruel outside. Should she have ventured out? Should she have opened the window and breathed the polluted air of their world? Maybe not. When she opened up to it, she was bitten and wounded by it. And permanently wounded…

The ugly face of hate and rage found its way into her and she cannot control it. It burns like a steady flame inside and feels like a bomb slowing ticking away. Tick, tick, tick….

Why is it that all she cannot tolerate now dwells in her world and invades it? And all that she wants and needs dwells just out of reach? She grows angrier…

She wants to erase herself and end the pain… NO! That won't do. That will never do. She must find the love that she once knew in her world and take it to theirs. That's the answer… Love.

A Mile in My Shoes

Allow me to introduce myself
I'm Miss Understood
You think you know me
Many people think they know me
But few actually do

Take a walk in my shoes
Do you know what it feels like
To wake up wishing you had died in your sleep?
Do you know how it feels
To look into a mirror and hate what you see?
And your biggest fear
Is that the world will see the same
And run away leaving you cold and alone?

Do you know how it feels
To wake up in the night
Startled by the sound of your own voice
Screaming, crying
Wondering why your own father walked away
Why your own mother only stuck around for a year
Then packed her bags leaving you crying behind her?
Do you know how it feels
To spend your entire life never fitting in?
Never feeling that you belong anywhere?
Constantly being told you're not good enough?
Do you?

Do you know how it feels to fear going to school
Because you fear being assaulted by your own classmates?
Do you know how it feels to fear being yourself
Because your own family doesn't understand you
And constantly tells you that everything that you are
Is crazy, incomprehensible?

Do you know how it feels to love someone
With all your heart and soul
To want him more than anything in life?
Do you know how it feels
To have his child.... after he has left you
Upon news that your beautiful child is on the way?
To have him come back and make you believe
That you'll finally be a family.....
Only for him to marry someone else?
Do you?

Well I do. I know all too well.
I know how it feels to feel ugly and inadequate
To not want to live anymore because I feel so unloved at times
But I also know how it feels
To have a child look up to me and think the world of me
I know how it feels to see true beauty in someone
And want to share my world with that person
And still trust even through ups and downs
And those are the moments that make life worth living
And those are the moments that allow me to keep moving forward

Part 1: *Stolen Innocence*
Written 6/20/07

Through darkness I feel a chill of fear
As I feel him coming near
I pretend to sleep hoping he will pass me by
I wipe the tears from my eyes
He's a predator and I'm his chosen prey
So I hold my breath, "Not again" I pray
My pleas seem unheard as he proceeds
To fulfill his selfish needs
Torn apart, I'm filled with anger
I'm his flesh; he treats me like a stranger
Ripping into my very soul
Making my heart turn cold
Who gave him the right to do this to me
I bite my lip; I pray to be set free
He has torn me apart, I'm wounded and cold
He has stolen a part of my very soul

I'm no longer a child, a woman before my time
He's the perpetrator, but I feel I've committed the crime
I comb the streets looking to be fulfilled
Desperate to find love, desperate to be healed
"Please, love me! Accept me!" that is my plea
But it seems all they want is my body
They take a part of me and throw me aside
My innocence is lost, and so is my pride
I'm searching, unfulfilled, wanting to be loved
I don't find it here so I look above

Part 2: *A Life Redeemed*

I reject the dream sellers, selling broken dreams
I search within to find my self-esteem
I'm not just a body, I'm a beautiful girl
I have a place in this world

9

So I put the past behind, press ahead and strive
And realize what it means to be fully alive
I'm a child of God, something greater than flesh
I see now that life was putting me to a test

So I reach out to Jesus' loving arms, He hears my story
And I know now to give Him glory
I may not understand why I endured such pain
But I now know that sunshine follows rain
I stood my test, and left a great testimony
I pray that you learn and grow from my story
I reached for Jesus' arms and he heard my cry
And took me up beyond the sky

Dedicated to A.J.
Sunrise: 8/27/1988 – Sunset: 7/2/2006

"Blood Pact"
Written 8/14/06

She writes his name, and wears it like a tattoo
"What is she thinking?" she overhears her friends
But she doesn't care
He is part of her
Her pen is a razor; her canvas is her own skin
She writes his name
And wears it as a tattoo
A promise that she will always be his
Even if he never sees her that way

Inspired by "T"... I heard you and I understand.

"Who?"
Written 11/08/2006

Who is this person that I've become

This isn't who I planned to be

When I look in the mirror I don't recognize

This person looking back at me

Broken into so many pieces

I feel there's nothing left

Can somebody help me find me I'm lost

And I'm holding on to my last breath

*This is actually the hook of a song that I recently wrote. I'm in the studio
now working on songs for my new album.*

"False Friend"

You think because I keep my cool
That I don't see who you really are
But I'm no fool

You think I'll believe whatever you tell me
Name dropping to impress but I can see
Your smile hides your deceit and lies

So cold.... but I know the truth
And remember karma bites hard

Untitled
Written 8/14/06

She hears a voice cry out for help
It wakes her in the night, shatters her peace
Desperation in her voice, she feels the sadness
The tears don't stop, she hears a voice crying
Trying to regain innocence lost
Trying to grab hold of her dreams
Trying to be whole again
She hears the screams, she feels the pain
Then she gets up and looks into the mirror
She notices tear stains
And realizes the voice she's been hearing
Is her own

*To those who are living with depression... I understand. This poem is
extremely personal for me. It's an everyday battle and at times it
feels almost impossible.... But there is a light at the end of the tunnel.
Giving my life to God has enabled me to win the fight one
battle at a time.*

"One Last Dance"
Written 7/3/2006

Dedicated Adrienne "A.J." Harding
8/27/1988 - 7/2/2006

People ask me why I do the things I do
Step inside my world and let me show you
I dance because when I dance I'm free
When I dance people see me for me
I dance because I long to be free
To escape the hands that abused me
I fantasize to escape the pain
I dance so that I can maintain
Step into my world and see
That all I want is for you to love me

People wonder why I say the things I do
Step inside my world and let me show you
Real life caused pain, but in my fantasy
My prince would come and he would love me
I dance because I long to be free
To escape the abuse that scarred me
I fantasize to escape reality
I dance because when I dance I'm free
Step into my world and see
That all I want is for you to love me

Through joy and pain, smiles and tears
I learned to work through all my fears
I came to realize that to be free
All I had to do was be me
To live to the fullest and love unconditionally
And then I could see that someone really loves me
Don't cry my family, my love is still here
Smile for me, wipe away your tears
My Father has called me home I'm finally free
And One Sweet Day you will be here dancing with me

"To My Friend Tasha"
Written 11/13/1997

A heart that's true
A smile so warm
A kind word or deed
In the midst of a storm

Beauty skin-deep
Is only a part
The true beauty of you
Is your genuine heart

So deep the loss
The pain severe
To now realize
That you're no longer near

The memories I'll cherish
Until we meet again
As you rest in Jesus' loving arms
My sister, my friend

To know you is to love you
A truer friend no one could find
You gave of yourself – heart, soul and mind

No one will ever know
The pain or fear that you endured
Bur your light still shone through brightly
You were strong and self-assured

Though they were not public
Many tears were shed
Fears and feelings of being unsure
Sometimes allowed you to be misled

But now as angels surround you
And lead you to Heaven's door
I pray The Lord washes away your pain
And grants you peace forever more

Dedicated to Tasha (11/3/75-11/12/97)

"Never.... Enough"
Written 6/29/2006

All my life I've been told I'm not ____ enough
In school I wasn't black enough to hang with the black girls
I wasn't white enough to hang with the white girls
I wasn't pretty enough to hang with the pretty girls
I wasn't odd enough to hang with the misfits
So I spent my days alone

When I got older I thought I'd found true love
But I wasn't domestic enough so I had to tone down my style
When I didn't react to his satisfaction he spoke with his hands
I had to be just ____ enough or I'd be punished
I suffered in silence until I'd had enough
And I moved on

Then I thought I'd found love, true love this time
I had the child I never thought I could have
And I wanted us to be a family
But I wasn't strong enough, I wasn't glamorous enough
So he chose someone else

Now here I am again... giving my heart to someone
Who doesn't even have a clue how much he means to me
But he won't take it because I'm not young enough
Not slim enough
Not pretty enough
Not "celeb status" enough
I watch my hopes fade away

Will I ever be good enough?

"My Angel"

I know angels are real
Because God brought you to me
I wouldn't be here without you
You gave us our roots
Now God has given you your wings

Dedicated to my Grandma Dorothy E. Queen
2/12/1928 - 4/12/2006

*I wrote this at my Grandma's bedside, about 2 hours after she passed away.
She was more than my Grandma, she was more like a mother to me. We had
an unmistakable bond, and I miss her terribly.*

Music Is the Heartbeat

I sang my first song at the age of 3, and wrote my first song at the age of 5. I remember being 4 year's old, standing on the coffee table in my living room using a hairbrush for a microphone and singing all the songs on the radio. I put on concerts for my neighborhood when I was 12, and in high school I entered every talent show I could. I performed everywhere possible – clubs, school, church, anywhere I could sing there I was. ☺ Music became a deep part of my life at an early age.

I gave it up for a while and realized that I was miserable without writing and performing. So I decided to go back to my passion… and this time nothing will make me let it go.

Music Is the Heartbeat

We're only passing through this world
On a spiritual journey
Music is the heartbeat
And love makes the trip worthwhile

written when I was 15 years old

This Music Thing
8/2/2007

I lived my life blind
Suffered words unkind
Struggling to mold myself
Into the person I "should" be
Given a gift, but unable to let it shine
Given pats on the back
But told my light will never shine
"Why not?" I ask
"Let it go, move on.
Find a 9 to 5 with a 401(K).
You're smart, you may even retire early
Put your college education to use.
Forget this music thing."

WHAT??!!??!!

This "music thing" is what makes me... ME
My music is like the air I breathe
It flows through my veins
Gives me life
This "music thing" is my purpose in life
My heart and soul, but yet I'm told
"For every star in Hollywood there's a thousand broken hearts."
"You don't have 'the look' to be a star."
"What makes you think YOU will ever be a star?"

WHAT??!!??!!

Who said I'm in it to be a "star"?
I'm an ARTIST
Creating images through words
Baring my soul, sharing stories
Painting pictures, touching hearts
I do this for the love of it

I don't care to be a "star"
I'll sing until I take my last breath
Write until there are no words left
And if I never make it to BET, VH1, or MTV
If I live in a 2-bedroom apartment
And never make it to MTV Cribs
If I never ship platinum like Beyonce
And push a bucket all my days
I'll be fulfilled
If I can touch someone, if I can reach someone
If my words can inspire someone
The way Patti LaBelle, Angela Bofill, Patrice Rushen, Alicia Keys, Janet
Jackson, Deniece Williams, Nikki Giovanni, Maya Angelou, Teena Marie,
Angie Stone, Jill Scott, Erykah Badu, and so many others have inspired me
Then this "music thing" is more than worth the time
You judge what you don't understand
Speak to what you do not know
Think you know when in reality you never can
My soul is healed by this "music thing"
This "music thing" takes away the pain
I'm an artist, not bound by the corporate world's chains
I'm finally free
Because I finally see
Just what this "music thing" truly means to me

Lights Camera Action
5/8/2007

For some the show begins
When the spotlight is on
Cameras are rolling
And the Director yells "Action!"
Or when the music begins to play
But for me the reverse is true
When the spotlight goes off
And I leave the stage
My real show begins
I pretend to be happy
Pretend all is well
Pretend I don't love him
Pretend I'm not wounded
Pretend to be content behind a desk
When my heart is in my songs
I pretend not to feel empty
Crying out to be filled
Longing to go back to my reality
Onstage sharing my feelings
Sharing my lyrics
Letting my true self shine
In all her glory
The real me comes through
Appreciated and heard
My words come to life through the speakers
I feel the presence of life
The presence of love
The presence of true happiness
Then and only then I can be myself
Not judged, not acting, not pretending
But full, whole and alive
But when the spotlight dims
And the music stops
I put on my mask
And pretend to be free
Until the next song I sing
Then I can truly be me

"Foolish Dream"
Song lyrics

Verse 1:
There's so much that I want you to know
But sometimes the words don't come easy
In my heart you're all that I need
Baby I reach out to you

If you knew
Just how much I love you
Would you feel the same for me?
Only time will tell

Chorus:
In your arms I wanna be
Tell me am I wasting my time on a foolish dream
Is this just a fantasy
Or is there a chance for you and me

Verse 2:
I close my eyes and I see your smile
Could it be infatuation?
A teenage dream still locked in my heart?
No baby you're much more to me

If I could
Open up my heart
and let you feel the love inside
You would understand

Repeat Chorus Twice

© 1999 J'Wan Yvette

"Baby You"
Song lyrics

Verse 1:
Your smile is what makes me happy
Your love makes me feel alive
I know I can touch the sky
You're my inspiration
And though I've loved before
This time I know it's real
Cuz you've shown a special love to me
That my heart has never known

Chorus:
Baby you are the wind beneath my wings
Baby you are my shining star
Baby you are with me in my heart
Whether you're near or far
Don't you know you're the one that I'm dreaming of
Wanna share my whole life with you
Yes you came into my world and made it new
Baby you

Bridge:
I'm writing you this letter from the heart
And though we can't be together now we'll never be apart
Never in our hearts
Baby you....

Repeat Chorus Twice

Dedicated to S.O.S. (From high school days)

"Closer to You"
Song lyrics

Chorus:
I wanna be closer to you
In every way
Can't you see what you mean to me
Say you'll always stay
I wanna be closer to you
Each and every day of my life
You're everything I need

Verse 1:
Did you ever feel
Like you've found a living dream
All the love you'll ever need
The one that makes you feel complete
I can say that I've found in you
The fantasy I've always had
You've been a friend through good and bad
And now (and now)
We'll watch our friendship grow
Into a special love
For only us to know

REPEAT CHORUS

Verse 2:
Now is the time
For us to become one
To make the dreams we dream come true

And I can't wait to hold you
My man (my man)
Say you'll always be
The one who'll be right by my side
Cuz I could never say goodbye
Tonight (tonight)
We'll let our hearts be free
We'll share a special love
Baby come to me

REPEAT CHORUS TWICE

© 1997 J'Wan Yvette

"Get With You"
Song lyrics

Was it the swagga that caught me
Held me captive to you
Since the first day
All I can think of is you
I got every reason to say no to you
But I dunno why all I can see is you
Ya smile
Ya style
Ya walk
Ya talk
Every little thing makes me drawn to you
Baby oh baby
What you do to me
I'm usually shy but when it comes to you

chorus:
I wanna hold you, wanna feel you
Gotta be real with u
Everything you do
Makes me wanna get with u
I wanna touch you, wanna kiss you
Every day I'm missin you
Everything you do
Makes me wanna get with u

Any given day a million numbers come my way
But the only one I wanna call is you
Am I losin my head
What is this feelin that's come over me
I got every reason to say no to you
But I dunno why all I can see is you
Ya style
Ya smile
Ya walk
Ya talk
Even your imperfections are perfect to me
Baby oh baby

What u do to me
U may never know what you do but still I sing this song to you

REPEAT CHORUS

INSTRUMENTAL BREAK

chorus:
I wanna hold you, wanna feel you
Gotta be real with u
Everything you do
Makes me wanna get with u
I wanna touch you, wanna kiss you
Every day I'm missin you
Everything you do
Makes me wanna get with u
(Repeat)

"What Could It Be"
My first commercial single – released October 2007

Verse 1:
What could it be that keeps me hooked up on you
Sittin by the phone hopin you call
Keep tryin to tell myself that you're the man for me
But in the end I mean nothing at all
What could it be that makes me stand up for you
When you never once stood up for me
But yet and still I keep on runnin back to you
By lovin you I'm steady losin me

What is it baby that makes me hold on
I can't remember the good times no more
What is it baby that keeps me holdin on
When I know you're no good for me
What is it baby that makes me hold on
I'm lost inside you and I've lost myself
This blind devotion is killin me
I need to move on and find someone else

Chorus:
(What could it be) Is it the way you hold me?
(What could it be) Is it the way you love me?
(What could it be) Is it the way you touch me?
(What could it be) What could it be baby?
(What could it be) Is it the way you love me?
(What could it be) Is it the way you hold me?
(What could it be) Is it the way you kiss me?
(What could it be) What could it be baby?

Verse 2:
What will it take for me to let go of you
What will you do that makes me finally break free
How many times will I put up with you
Before I get tired of you hurting me
What will it be that makes me let go of you
What will it take for me to walk away
How many times must my heart be broken

By all these silly little games you play

What is it baby that makes me hold on
I can't remember the good times no more
What is it baby that keeps me holdin on
When I know you're no good for me
What is it baby that makes me hold on
I'm lost inside you and I've lost myself
This blind devotion is killin me
I need to move on and find someone else

Chant:
Ladies if you're tired of him breakin your heart tell him
"It's time to move on, it's time to move on!"
If you can't take the games he's playin on you tell him
"It's time to move on, it's time to move on!"
Ladies if you're tired of him breakin your heart tell him
"It's time to move on, it's time to move on!"
If you can't take the games he's playin on you tell him
"It's time to move on, it's time to move on!" – What!

REPEAT CHORUS

The Journey to Love Myself

For too long, depression stole moments in my life. Little by little, it was robbing me of happiness, love, and of life itself. I went through bouts of self-hate and doubt, until I found my one true anti-depressant: JESUS CHRIST. The road was long and sometimes very difficult, but I'm living proof that there is life after depression. And it is oh, so sweet!

For a long time, I thought that I would find happiness in a certain man.... Ladies, we've all been there. We've all that moment that we thought that one special man would be our end all and be all. But I found that the answer was not him... it was within me. Learning to trust God and love myself became the answer.

This section explores the journey, from the lows to the highs and everything in between. To anyone out there who has struggled with depression, or knows someone who is struggling with it, know that you are not alone. And there is hope.

Screaming
4/21/2007

She's screaming on the inside
Tears flowing like an endless river
She's been broken and torn
Seeking shelter from the storms
She has loving family and friends
So why does she feel cold and alone?
The screams become louder
More desperate, more painful
"Make the pain stop, please"
She begs silently to him
But he doesn't hear
He's unaware that he's her cure
He's unaware that only he can take away the pain
And make her feel whole again
He's unaware that even a word from him
Eases her suffering and brings a smile 2 her face
So he remains just out of her reach
And she mourns for a love that never was
Watches herself bleed as she tries to silence
The cries and screams within her
She knows that her dreams will never become reality
There will never be a happy ending
He will never see her the way she sees him
So she patiently waits for the day
That she is free from her body
And can soar to the clouds

"Unbeautiful"
6/12/2007

I'm told that I'm beautiful
But when I look in the mirror
I don't see what they see
I don't see any beauty
In the image staring back at me
The models that grace magazine covers
Are tall and thin and magnify everything
I wish I could be
According to Cosmo, I'll never be en vogue
The beautiful people will never accept me
My hair doesn't flow flawlessly down my back
My skin is not like porcelain, my features are not dainty
And do you see this body fitting into a size 2?
Just for one day I'd love to be
One of the beautiful people
One of the ladies that men would give anything for
One of the ladies that girls aspire to be
Then maybe my dreams could be reality
At least for that day I wouldn't hear things like,
"You have a pretty face..."
So I'd be acceptable if I were a head, is that what you mean?
Too bad society doesn't see inner beauty
If people could see the real me, who I am inside
Then maybe I wouldn't feel so unbeautiful

Being overweight in a society that tells you that anything over a size 4 is unbeautiful has been a struggle. As a teenager I was 5'8" and a size 14... and hated it. My weight has fluctuated and so has my attitude about it. But now that I'm older and wiser I realize that being a size 18 doesn't make me less of a woman, just as melting down to a size 4 won't make me a better person. I've learned to accept myself, just as I am. And I love the skin I'm in!

MissUnderstood
4/19/2007

Allow me to introduce myself
I'm MissUnderstood
You think that you know me
But in reality you never could
You take my down days as laziness
My confusion for a game
If you knew the truth about me
You'd understand my name
If only I could show you
What I go through day to day
How I wish I could shake these thoughts
And make them go away
Do you know how it feels
To wake up each morning new
Wishing you could be
Anyone else but you
When you're being told to be yourself
Then crucified for doing so
To be ridiculed and kicked
By nearly everyone you know
To not understand
Your own thoughts inside
To look in the mirror
And want to run and hide
To love someone dearly
And know that they'll never know
To have to realize
That your dreams you must let go
Allow me to introduce myself
I'm MissUnderstood
You think you know me
But in reality you never could

Be Yourself
8/25/2006

They say "be yourself"
But that's not what they mean
No one wants you to be yourself
They want you to be what they want you to be
Be yourself until your true self
Doesn't fit their image
Be yourself until they don't understand you
Be yourself until being yourself
Makes them uncomfortable
Be yourself... what a joke
No one wants you to truly be yourself
They want to fit their expectations
And when you don't fit their expectations
They analyze, criticize
They don't want you to be yourself
They only want to you fit their image of what you should be

Work In Progress
7/15/2007

Be patient, God's still working on me
I long for freedom but I'm not yet free
He's molding me into the woman I'll be
A butterfly that will fly and be free
Be patient, God isn't finished with me
He's molding me into the mother I should be
He's molding me into the friend I should be
The daughter and sister that He would have me be
Be patient, God is working on me
Building my patience, creating a new spirit in me
Taking away fear, easing the pain
Bringing me a rainbow after the rain
So be patient, I'm a work in progress
Learning from my failures to work toward success
God is the Light guiding me, keeping me warm
Sheltering me in the time of storm

I stumbled and fell, but now I'm firm on my feet
And I know that's because of God's love inside me
Things that once shook me no longer faze me
For God's love and grace are here to sustain me
I'm not perfect, and will not be
But I'm a better person because God lives in me
I'm stronger and am no longer beaten down
By words and rumors people use to try and bring me down
Be patient, God is working on me
Creating a new spirit of love inside me
Taking away the fear that once controlled me
I'm confident that now those chains can't hold me
Please be patient, I'm a work in progress
Learning from my failures to work toward success
God is the Light guiding me, keeping me warm
Sheltering me in the time of storm

Mother and Child

February 3, 2000 was the day that changed my life for the better. That was the day I became a mother. Three different doctors told me at three different times that I would never be a mother… that even if I did become pregnant, the baby wouldn't grow to term. But at 6:34 p.m. on February 3, 2000, God proved them all wrong. Jessica was born happy and healthy; a full-term baby who weighed in at 9 pounds and 21 inches long. I never knew that I could love anyone so much… being a mother made me understand the true meaning of love. This section is dedicated to my princess, Jessica Mollie-Gabrielle.

"Jessica"
Written 2/4/2000

Thank God for you
An angel so sweet
A gift I never thought would be
I named you Jessica
Because you're a living testimony
Of God's grace
I have a reason to live
To the fullest
Love to the maximum
When I thought all was lost
And when man said "No"
God said "Yes"
And gave me a beautiful daughter
Thank God for this gift
My precious Jessica

Daughter
8/2/2007

I know how to love because of you
I'm a better person because I love you
I know how it feels to be loved
When you look at me
A beautiful reflection of two become one
"My daughter"... how proud I am to say those words!
I'm a better me
Because I'm your mother

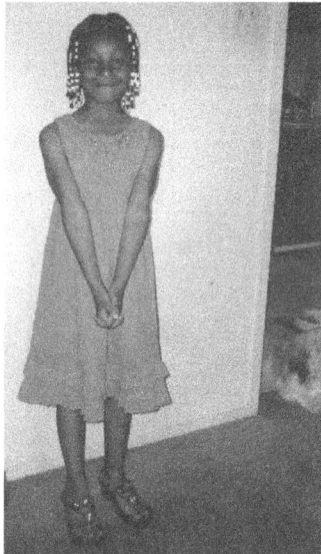

For My Princess
8/2/2007

Dream big, my love
One day those dreams will be reality
You were born to be larger than life
A gift to the world
Some say you're spoiled
But how else should a Princess be treated?
You are strong and already wiser than your years
Don't fear, my love
Mommy is here to guide you
To teach you, reassure you, and nurture you
To dry your tears, pick you up when you fall
Never doubt that I'll give you my all
There's no storm that God, you, and I can't face together
Take my hand, and we will take His
And one day our dreams will come true
Sleep well tonight, my love
A new dawn is coming soon
This is only a test
One day we will have a testimony
One day my Princess will be a light for the world
You will be a Queen
So hold your head high, my love
Know that you are truly loved
God is working through you
And you will teach others how to love
You are a child of God
A gift to the world
Dare to dream big, and don't fear, my love
Your dreams will come true

Through Jessica's Eyes
6/20/07

For one day I'd love to see the world through her eyes
Explore the possibility of one day becoming a Basketball
Player/Actress/Model/Football Coach/Office Assistant/Singer/Hairdresser
who loves candy, cartoons and traveling
To heal all wounds with a Band-Aid and a kiss
To believe that everything in the world is good
And bad can be erased with just the right amount of chocolate
Or the right pizza
Or maybe just good old fashioned TLC
To know that your only care in the world is what kind of waffles you'll
have for breakfast
And what games you'll play with your friends at recess
To one moment have a crush on a teeny bop singer and imagine dates at
fictional restaurants
Then decide that you only like him as a friend because you're much too
young to "like him like him"
The bliss of childhood
Moments so pure and unspoiled
Still innocent, untouched by the cynicism of the world
To live those days again
I can't go back
But I thank God that I can watch my daughter live those moments
Moment by moment I remember innocence

Romantic Love, Fantasy, and Crushes

When I fall in love, I tend to give 125% of myself. That's not always a good thing… but it makes for great poetry. ☺ Many of the poems in this section were inspired by a special someone in my life; someone I've admired for quite a while and recently I've been blessed to count him among my friends. He's my muse.

Some of the poems in this section are based on dreams, fantasies, and situations that I've experienced in life or some that I've seen others go through. Love can be a strange thing at times… yet in the end when it's true; it's more than worth the battles we sometimes face.

Complete
5/4/2007

I was looking for him to complete me...
When suddenly I realized...
I'm complete all by myself.
So instead I'd like for us
To simply compliment each other.

My Love
7/3/2007

I used to go searching for love
Wanting to be fulfilled
Wanting to feel what it's like to be loved
Someday my prince will come I've been told
So I searched for him endlessly
Wanting to fulfill my need
My longing to be loved
Then I saw him
Everything I could ever want
Beauty personified, I knew he'd be the one
My love, my prince
No scratch that... my King
My everything
But he's out of my reach
Close enough to touch, yet so far away
So patiently I wait
I wait for the right way
And the right time
To tell him that I love him
That I'd sacrifice everything for him
That I'd do anything to please him
That I'm patiently waiting
Other guys may try
But I don't answer their calls
I leave them standing
Because it's for him I wait
Moments with him I treasure
Memories so sweet, if only fleeting moments
It's for him and only him that I wait
Only to him will I give my love

Love Turns to Hate

I hate you
Because my love for you has become a shield
It prevents me from letting anyone else in
Fear and insecurity live where love once did
I gave it to you freely
And you misused and abused it
Took it for a joke
Tossed me aside when I no longer served your purpose

What hurts the most is
You never truly let me in
Your lies were pretty
Dishonesty dressed up in poetic words
Leading my heart closer to you
Leading me to give you more of myself
Until there was nothing left to give
Only to find that my love was a joke in your eyes
I never had a chance to make it real
And I was the last to know

Now my love has turned to hate
Insecurity and fear live where love once did
I try to move on, but fear rules me
Afraid to open my heart and love again
Always afraid that a new man's words
Will end up in the same pain and anger I feel now
I sabotage my own happiness
To avoid my heart being broken again
By another man like you

I once loved you with all my heart
But now it's torn apart
Will I ever love again?
Will I continue to punish myself and any man who comes near?
For the lies you told?

For the pain you caused?

Love is blind
And I was blind
Now I see, but I hate what I see
I've been a fool, hoping for something that would never happen
Now I'm left empty
Fear and insecurity now live where love once did
Will I ever feel love again?
And if I do, will he feel the same?

Unbreakable
3/30/2007

I wish my heart were unbreakable
I built a wall determined never to let anyone in
My wall protected me from harm
Then you came along
My wall began to crumble
I fought with all my might
I tried not to let you in
But you slowly sank under my skin
You crept into my dreams
Into my thoughts
Right into my very soul
You penetrated my wall with a smile
Gave me the sweetest fantasies
The most incredible dreams
Made me fly like a bird in the sky
Such beautiful dreams
Then reality awakens me
It's only a fantasy
Reality reminds me that I'm still alone
You were next to me in my dream
But when I open my eyes I'm in my bed alone
Reaching out for someone who isn't there...
And never will be
I wish my heart were unbreakable
Then I wouldn't have to rebuild this wall
To protect my heart
From loving you so deeply

Why?
9/19/2006

Why is it so hard for you to make up your mind
One minute you're hers the next you're mine
I want to let go but my heart is in your hands
But when I think we're there, it slips through my hands
What must I do to let you my love is real
What else will it take to show you how I feel
What does she have that keeps you running to her
What will it take to make you forget her?

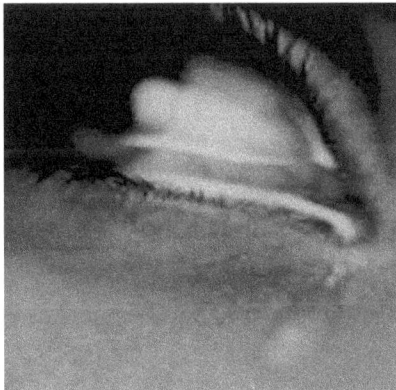

I Care For You
5/2/2007

I'm not sure how to define it
Sometimes I think "love" is too strong a word
I try to convey my feelings
But still I'm left unheard
If I tell you I care would you listen?
Or would you still have doubts?
If I take it slow will you let me in
Or continue to keep me out?
I tell myself this is crazy
But you're always on my mind
I'm still consumed with thoughts of you
And these feelings are undefined
Too strong to be friendship, too distant to be love
I guess it's somewhere in between
I know we can never be a true "us"
But each night you're still in my dreams
So I guess I'm ending just where I started
On the outside looking in
Still holding on, hanging on every word
Hoping one day you'll let me in
Praying that you'll see I'm not like them
I love you for the real you
Even if the fame, money and looks one day fade
I'll always still care for you

Worlds Apart
6/20/07

In reality we are worlds apart
Yet I reach out and touch you in my dreams
When you open the door and give me a glimpse
The reality of you and me is closer than it seems
Why does it feel so right to give you my heart
When I'm a stranger in your eyes
Yet every day I draw closer to you
Convinced you're my angel in disguise
When my heart is broken you're my only cure
My defense against the cold world
Yet all odds and logic tell me I'll never be your girl
Still I hold on, hanging on your every word
When I hear from you I smile
All it takes is a simple "hello" to make the wait worthwhile
The sound of your voice brings me pure joy
Your smile makes my heart dance
Just to be friends with you makes my soul happy
I'm so glad I took the chance
Even though on the surface we're worlds apart
Deep down we are closer than we know
I feel blessed to have you as a friend
And I look forward to watching our friendship grow

Rhyme or Reason
Written 5/2/2007

Where is the rhyme or reason
In this so-called love?
Can I even call it love
When I'm chasing someone
Who gives me no reciprocity?
Every fiber of my being
Cries out for him
But reality and my practical mind
Tell me this is insane

"He doesn't love you!
He won't!
He can't!"

Thoughts of him fill my mind all day
Dreams of him flood my subconscious all night
Yet I truly doubt that he even remembers
That he met me
I tell myself f I only try harder
Transform myself into what he likes
Maybe, just maybe...
Then my practical mind screams

"He doesn't love you!
He won't!
He can't!"

I drown in my tears
Only to be resurrected by a word from him
Only words typed over cyberspace
But it's enough to breathe life
Into my broken heart
Maybe he sees something in me
Maybe he understands how much I love him

Then that nagging voice
Shatters my maybes

"He doesn't love you!
He won't!
He CANNOT!"

Tears again fill my eyes
As I realize it's a dream
Only a dream
A fantasy captured in my heart
He doesn't love me.
He won't.
He can't.

But I still love him
Refuse to let anyone else in
Because no one can replace him
Refuse to trust anyone but him
Where is the rhyme or reason?
Why can't my heart say no?
Let go?
Stop this painful cycle?
Where is the rhyme or reason?
Love shouldn't hurt this way.

"Close To You"
6/12/07

I'm told to let you go, that you're a fantasy
But they don't know you're my reality
I'm inspired to sing because of your smile
I'm inspired to step up my game because of your style
I'm inspired to move forward when I'm knocked 2 steps back
And it's because of you that I press on
I don't know why, but I feel so close to you
As if we met in another lifetime
I see my future in your eyes and forever in your smile
Am I crazy to go that extra mile
To work hard to be my very best just for you
To push away all the other dudes that try
Because for me no one else will do
Am I crazy to feel so close to you
When miles and years create such a distance
Still I have tunnel vision, all I see is you
Though you don't see my persistence
I don't have much but I'd give all I have
Just to show you how deep my feelings are for you
You've got it all but I'd give you the world and more
Just to show you that no one could love you more
If I had the world at my feet I'd give it away
If giving it away would bring me closer to you

Pleasure Meets Pain
8/8/07

I look at him I see my king
The love of my life, my everything
But all chances are he will never be mine
And I'm told my love will fade with time
But 2 years, 6 months my love is still strong
Who would have thought it would last this long
Yet even though we speak from day to day
I continue to feel pushed away
I love him in ways that no one else can
But when he looks at me he sees a "fan"
He sees my love for him, yet I doubt he'll ever see
The day that he can give me reciprocity
I can't make him love me, I can't force him to see
Just how much he truly means to me
I try to connect to him, try to be his friend
Constantly wondering if our communication will end
"He's just being nice because he doesn't want to hurt you"
"You must be crazy if you think he'll ever love you"
Crazy I must be, my heart won't let go
I dream of him every night when deep down I know
He and I will never be more than friends
He will never see me as a potential girlfriend
Yet when other guys try, my heart won't say yes
Because I refuse to settle for less than the best
There is no one else, he's the king of my heart
For over 2 years now, he has ruled my heart
This kind of love doesn't just fade away
And in my heart he will always stay
I'll make the sacrifice and be alone for life
No substitute will do, I'll sacrifice being a wife
Or lover to any other man besides him
Never again will I let someone else in
My love for him won't let me move on
So for him I'll sing my greatest song

I'd rather have him as a friend than nothing at all
I'll continue to close the door on any guy who calls
Loving him is my pleasure, my shelter from the rain
Knowing he doesn't love me back is the source of my pain
But the good outweighs the bad, he is my friend
And that's a bond I'll treasure till the end
Is it truly better to have loved and lost what's yours
Or to love someone knowing they will never, ever be yours?
That question I ponder but in the end
It doesn't matter... all I know is I love him

The Chase

He dreamed of her… the most beautiful woman on earth. Her skin was like milk; her eyes were mysterious, but alluring. He wanted to touch her, but she danced just out of her reach. In the night, he saw her… but not in a dream this night. She danced for him, yet seemed to ignore his presence. He wanted to hold her, but she danced just out of his reach. His eyes explored every part of her…her every feature exposed, but forbidden to him. She remained silent.

Each night she'd dance for him and each night she'd disappear without a word spoken. "I want to love you," he begged. She didn't respond. He needed her. He begged to hold her, love her. She danced away.

Deep in the night, her presence awakened him. He needed her more than ever. "I want to love you," he begged. She continued to dance. His pulse raced as thoughts of her in his arms invaded his mind. He reached for her, but this time she couldn't dance away. He held her, but she resisted. She didn't speak to him – she fought to escape his arms. As his lips brushed her cheek, she screamed in protest and once again she disappeared. She didn't return.

He remained lost on the fine line between fantasy and reality…his love for her never ended. But who was she? What was she? If it was only his imagination, he didn't care. He knew that he loved her… He wanted her to dance for him again. She never returned…..

You May Not Have My Number
8/2/2007

No, you may not have my number; I don't want to know your name
Because I know guys like you, and you're all the same
I trusted you before, met you a thousand times
Just to find out you're all the same guy in disguise
I say "guy" and not "man" because a man would never do
The f***ed up things that you guys do
Spread your seed at will, then you're gone
Leaving another "baby mama" to make it on her own
Claim to love someone, make promises for life
Only for her to find out that you already have a wife
I see through the game, I recognize the lies
Just another snake in a 'Good Man' disguise
So no, you may not have my number; I don't care to know your name
Y'all dudes think you're slick, but you're all the same
See I guess I can blame myself for ever believing
There was just one man out there worth believing
But let's see, there was So and So back in high school
The one that used to play it so cool
Told me I was cute and he wanted the digits
But bounced when he asked for the V-card and I wasn't with it
Then there was Blahzay-Blah, yea he was tight
Met me on a cruise, said he was in love the same night
Promised to love me, and wife me, I thought he was it
Until he started expressing his "love" with his fists
Then there was the Dude, the one I fell for hard
Had me convinced he was my gift from God
I gave him my all, had his child, made him my life
Only to find that he already chose his wife
I gave up, moved on; trust was no longer an option
Took my broken heart through recovery, tried to heal then he got to me
Took my time, didn't want to get played ever again
So I took it slowly and became his friend
Little by little, he broke down my wall
Still not ready to give him my all

But I was ready to try, ready to feel good again
So foolishly I let him in
Four days, no call, not even a text
What was my heart in for next
Finally his number appeared on my caller ID
But it was not him... his lady wanted to speak to me
So my heart is closed, no longer able to feel
No longer able to open up, not again will anyone steal
What joy I have left, my heart is off limits
And so is everything else – So, no you won't get up in it
So no, you may not have my number, I don't care to know your name
Because guys like you are all the same
Trust no longer lives here, neither does love
Except for my family, my TRUES, and for The Lord Above

Written after thinking back to "M"... who wanted to 'show me what true love should feel like'... he conveniently left out the fact that he was engaged and living with his fiancé. And "D" who promised to love me and treat me as a treasure... only to show his "love" by physically and sexually abusing me, cheating on me and lying to me. And "E" who went out with me for over a year... and 6 months after our child was born he confesses that he was already engaged and had 3 kids. And lastly, "P" who gained my trust, talked about moving together and getting out of Maryland, and supporting my daughter and me so that I could pursue my career... then I found out he was attached and living with his significant other. This was written from a dark and bitter place, the way I felt the moment I heard "P"'s girlfriend's voice on the phone after having been duped so many times before. This poem would have been my reaction to any man who tried to talk to me at that moment. But even after dealing with immature little boys like these, I still believe there are good men left in this world.

Beautiful
3/30/2007

Captivated
Can't quite place what it is about him
But he is simply beautiful
His eyes are inviting
Dark, deep, emotional
But he appears so cool
His lips are inviting and sensual

Simply captivated
When I look at him everything else disappears
My sadness is released
My worst day becomes my best
All it takes is a smile
Or the sound of his voice

Beautiful
That's what he is to me
Simply beautiful
Breathtaking
Captivating
No one else compares
If only he knew what he means to me

"Without You"
Written 5/4/2007

I thought there was no me without you
I thought I couldn't move on without you
Died inside because I did not want to live without you
Cried day and night because I was lost without you
Spent all my days thinking about you
Spent all my nights dreaming about you
Even when you took time to talk to me I'd doubt you
Made every aspect of my life about you
Woke up in the night crying out your name
Silently sinking in my own shame
How do I go on without you
When every fiber of my being is dying without you

But then I realized through all my tears
Being without you is the least of my fears
I accomplished goals I set for myself without you
I'm a mother raising a beautiful daughter without you
I'm a sister, a friend, I can love without you
My dreams are coming true... and I did it without you
I'm a strong woman, with or without you
I realize that my life is not about you

I'm determined to be happy with or without you
I'm determined to be whole with or without you
I realize that my happiness is not defined by you
I can be happy and whole if I'm not beside you
And if the day comes that we are true friends
I'll treasure that friendship and love until the end
But if that day never comes I'll still think about you
And I'll still be happy.... with or without you

Something Beautiful Remains
5/2/2007

At times our words were unkind
At times our actions were immature
Our intentions were good
But sometimes our ways and means were not
What we think is love can sometimes make us do strange things
I have few regrets
Because every experience happened for a reason
And I've learned from my mistakes
And through all the drama
sorrow
highs
lows
ups
and downs
Something beautiful remains
And I'm glad our lives crossed paths
Because without us, there would be no her.
Thank you.

Dedicated to "Baby daddy"

With All My Heart
8/8/07

How can you love him?
You barely know him!
Why do you go so far to show him?
You write him letters, buy him things...
What has he done for you?

I smile and reply, "All he needs to do is be himself. That's enough for me."

You know he doesn't feel the same way
Yet you pour out your heart every day...
What about Soandso, Blazayblah, they call you
But you never call them back
Are you holding out for *HIM*?
Girl you need to let that go
It's a fantasy!
He's not buyin' you anything!
He's not shedding any tears for you!
He's not even someone you can be with for real.
What do you see in him?
How can you love him?

I smile and reply, "With all my heart."

"I Wish"

I wish I didn't care so much
I wish I could let go
You've become a part of me
Although you may not know
I tell myself to get over you
But my heart just won't let go
You're everything I could ever want
Just thought I'd let you know

"Why"

Why do I feel so close to you
When you're so far away
How can I imagine a future with you
When we barely had yesterday
Why do I see forever in your eyes
When you never even looked into mine
Now you've given your heart to her
And I feel that I've been left behind

Whatever she can give you I can give you more
I'm not hatin, just speaking the truth
I've done all I can to show you my love
But I guess there's just no use
I'm trying inside to be happy for you
Because I know your feelings for her are real
Eventually I'll have to make myself let go
And let my wounded heart heal

"Invisible"

In my heart he's My King
My love, my soul, my everything
But when he sees me I'm a face in the crowd
True connection is not allowed
If he looks into my eyes he'll see adoration
But I look into his, no sign of admiration
He's happy to see me because it's his gain
But I disappear from his mind until he sees me again
I wake up each morning with him on my mind
But does he think of me? I'm sure I'm not on his mind
I'm invisible to him, but he's all I see
What can I do to make him love me
My heart cries from all this pain
Holding on to the next time I'll see him again
Risking everything just for a moment with him
Maybe one day he'll see how much I love him
But I'm invisible to him, just a blur in the crowd
True connection is not allowed
Maybe if I looked like her he'd notice me
Maybe then he'd open his heart and see
My love for him is deeper than any sea
Wider than any ocean, overflowing inside me
I hold him up on a pedestal, My King
But to him, I'm invisible, I'm less than nothing
He's chosen his queen... I'm just a voice in the crowd
True feelings for me will never be allowed
I'm invisible to him, I'm just not there
Will he ever see how much I care?
I'm invisible to him, but he's all I see
What can I do to make him love me

"Broken"

I'm whole when I hear your voice
When I see you
When I think of you
Those are the moments that my world is complete
But when you're away
I'm broken
I'm torn
Wanting you, needing you
Knowing I can't have you
But still longing for you
Treasuring the moment no matter how brief
When our eyes met
When our fingertips touched
A smile
A wink
Idle conversation
The pieces come together and make me whole
But you're far away, those thoughts fade into yesterday
Now I'm left alone
And broken

"What's Missing"
Written 3/21/06

The sun brightened up my room
And my day began a new
All that was missing is a smile from you
I received good news
Heard from an old friend
All that was missing is having you to share it with
Even had a great lunch
Great conversation
All that was missing was a call from you
No matter where I go or what I do
There's an emptiness inside
That's only filled when I see you
When I'm near you
When I hear the sound of your voice
All that's missing in my life is you

"Damaged"

Broken into pieces
Shattered, a mess
2 years ago I was whole
Then I saw your face and I was hooked
Even before we met you captured my heart
I'd take one step closer
Then you'd take a million steps back
Or so it seems
Loving you has destroyed me
Pieces chipped away with every rejection
Pieces chipped away with every realization
That you'll never love me the way I love you
Pieces chipped away with every rumor of you
And her
Pieces chipped away when I realized
You'll never find me nearly as beautiful
As I find you
Pieces chipped away as I tried to move on
With someone else
Only to find that no one can replace you
So many pieces chipped away that there's nothing left
I can't be with anyone else
Because of my love for you
Yet you'll never see, you'll never love me
I'm trapped
My heart is broken
And I'm left damaged
And my fear is that only your love can repair me

"What If"
Written 3/4/2007

What if you weren't on TV
What if we just met on the street
And it was just you and me
What would you see in me?
Would you see in me what I see in you
Someone special that you'd give your time to
When I see you I see someone beautiful
Someone with whom I'd share my world
If not as your partner then as your friend
I'd be someone you can count on till the very end

What if you saw the real me, not just a face in the crowd
What if I could share my thoughts of you out loud
What if other people's opinions didn't matter
And I didn't have to stay inside my own shadow
What if I could get to know you
The real you, not just the image of you
What if you allowed me to be your friend
So this string of questions in my head could end
What if you knew that you make my heart sing
What if you knew that you're my everything

What if I shared my secrets with you
What if I told you that I pray for you
I pray for your success, for your happiness
I want to see you achieve the very best
You're a star in my eyes, not because of your fame
To me you'd still be a star without your money or name

I want to hold you down through thick and thin
Even if you found your queen, I'd be your best friend
To me you're a treasure beyond compare
What if I told you I'd always be there

What if all the other girls turned away
What if I told you I'd be there anyway
I'd cherish the day that we became friends
And treasure that day until the end
What if miles and years didn't create this distance
What if nothing mattered... would you hear my plea?
What if I told you I love you, would that scare you away?
Or would you know that I love you as a friend and stay
What if at the end of this illusion there is some peace
What if we were friends.... true friends, you and me.

"He Is My Drug"

I'm addicted
I never planned for it to be this way
My first hit took me to places I'd never been
High for days from just one hit
Feeling withdrawal from being without for a day
Ran back for another fix
What is this?
This isn't like me
Running city to city just for a chance
The smallest amount will do
Nothing else will do
My mind is gone... I'm no longer me
I'm a puppet on a string, controlled by this addiction
Confused, consumed by the smallest hit
Yet withdrawal is more than I can bear
My addiction is the first thought on my mind when I wake up
The last thought before I go to sleep at night
I try to let go, I go into rehab
But it never lasts more than a day
I'm feenin again, hungry for another hit
I'm cursed out by family and friends
Yet nothing is enough for me to let go
He is my addiction
He is my drug
Without him I'm broken
But with him I'm torn
I've come to the conclusion
That I'd rather be torn and have a piece of him
Than let go and have nothing at all

"Taking It Back"
Written 7/21/06

I gave all my love to you
Hoping it would be returned
I gave you my heart
Only to have it shattered and burned
What a fool I was
To make you my everything
To make you my world
When to you I mean nothing
What I thought I saw in you
Was a fantasy
So I'm taking that love back
Cuz I need it for me

Picking myself apart
To be beautiful to you
Changing everything I am
Just to look good for you
Changing everything I believe in
Just for a chance with you
Knowing inside
I shouldn't even want you
Investing so much emotion
In a love that wasn't meant to be
So I'm taking that love back
Cuz I need it for me

Falling apart at the seams
Wondering how to compete with her

Feeling jealous
Wanting to be like her
Just to be near you
Just to hold you one time
Just for a moment
To pretend you're mine
Crying myself to sleep
Night after night
Knowing inside
This can't be right
But no more (NAME DELETED)
I'm letting go
So one last time
I'm letting you know
I see now
That we were never meant to be
So I'm taking that love back
Cuz I need it for me

"How Ironic"
Written 1/29/2007

I try to get over him but he creeps into my dreams
I try to tell myself that he's all wrong for me
I try to let go and move on
I try not to love him
I try not to care
But it's been almost 2 years
And I love him more than ever
Think of him more than ever
Want him more than ever
Care for him more than ever
And he has no idea
If he fell off tomorrow I'd be there to catch him
If he lost everything I'd give him my last dime
So it's not his fame or his money that attract me
If his looks changed I wouldn't go anywhere
I'd do nothing but continue to love him and care
But he can't see that
I'm invisible to him even when I'm right in front of him
My love means nothing to him even though I'm giving him my heart
Why am I so stuck on him? Why can't I let go?
I'm stronger than this but he makes me weak
I'm smarter than this but I go stupid to prove my love for him
The thought of my life without him in it frightens me
But trying to hold on to any hope for an "us" is exhausting
I'm drowning in him.... and only his love can save me
How ironic.

"Puppet"
Written 1/24/2007

He holds the strings
My emotions are chained to him
I'm happy when he notices me
I'm sad when he doesn't care
I'm elated when we share a laugh
I'm torn when he isn't there
I'm lost I'm no longer me
I'm his puppet
My every emotion tied to him
He holds the strings
My heart is in his hands
I pray that he doesn't cut the ties
Or I'll be lost.......

I wrote this after about a month of talking to that someone that I'd become emotionally attached to…. Really talking to him not just an idle hello here and there like before. It's pretty interesting to read this now…a little scary aswel.

"Puppet - Part 2"
Written 2/19/2007

I was his puppet on a string
He controlled my every emotion
My happiness was chained to him
And for about 6 weeks
I was happy
He held the strings
And made me dance
But it turned out to be an illusion
Now I'm filled with confusion
He cut the strings
No life is left in me
I'm on the floor....
And I don't want to be picked up
Let me disappear
Without him I'm broken
Let me disappear
Without him happiness is a dream
Let me disappear
Without him I'm lifeless
I'm a puppet whose strings have been cut
My life has ended.

Written after a misunderstanding led to nearly 2 weeks of us not communicating... Good news is he realized it was a misunderstanding and we became friends again. And I also realized that maybe I'd become a little too attached. ☺ So from here on out, I resolve to have a healthier relationship with him... and with myself.

"I Hate You"
Written 12/12/2006

I hate you for what you've done to me
I hate you cuz I can't seem to break free
I hate you for holding me and kissing me
I hate you for being there for me
I hate you because you're forcing me to let you go
When your love and your touch is all I want to know
I hate the fact that you're falling for someone new
Most of all I hate myself for still loving you

Dedicated to (he knows who he is). But I'm glad we're still friends.

"Empty"
Written 3/12/2007

Inside I'm empty
Looking to be filled
Abandoned and lost
Afraid
Then I saw him
He is beautiful
The most beautiful guy I'd ever seen
Perfect from head to toe
Even his imperfections to me were perfect
He filled me
Suddenly my heart was filled with love
My head filled with sweet memories
Of a love that never was
And could never be
But oh, such a sweet, sweet fantasy
No one could fill that spot
No one but him
I reach out, timid and afraid
Being mocked, being laughed at
But I didn't care - they don't understand me
They don't understand that when I see him
All the memories of abuse and abandonment leave me
My broken heart is mended
When I hear his voice my world is perfect
I'm no longer the child who was left behind
Or the girlfriend who was jilted for another
In my mind he knows me and sees me
The real me
The person inside who loves him
My love is real, it's pure
No matter how much the words of gossip chicks
Try to taint it
I hold on to that feeling because it keeps me going
When I see him, when I hear his voice
I'm no longer empty
He fills me with joy

Dedicated to *HIM*...

Puppet – Part 3
Written 3/12/2007

I need to break away
My emotions are tied to him
And I know this is unhealthy
When he turns away I'm lost
But all it takes is a single word
To bring a smile back to my face
Break the ties
Cut the strings
I want to breathe again
He became my life support
And I forgot about me
Forgot what makes me happy
Because all I wanted was HIM to make me happy
Break the ties
Cut the strings
I want to breathe again
I no longer want to be his puppet
Let my heart beat again
Break the ties
Cut the strings
I want him to be my friend
Not my puppet master

I wrote this after I resolved to have a healthier relationship with him… and with myself.

"More Than a Crush"
Written in 2003

I never knew I could feel this way
You may think what I feel is just a crush
But it is so much more
You are perfection in motion to me
Your beautiful eyes, your sensuous lips
Your perfectly masculine body
But your physical features are only icing on the cake
Your true beauty lies within
Your kind and caring heart is what captured me
You hold my heart in your hands
Though you may not know it
I dream of you every night
And I awaken longing to hold you near
When I'm down thoughts of you lift my spirits
I long for the day I can call you mine

Inspired by "D". I still remember our chats… I miss those days. ☺

"If These Walls Could Talk"

If these walls could talk
My secrets they would tell
The endless tears I cry
The way I'm under your spell
The way my heart races
At the sound of your name
Since you came into my life
I know I'll never be the same
They would tell how I miss you
When the time goes by
How I dream of kissing you
I just don't know why
I can't shake these feelings
I thought it was a crush
But just a simple thought of you
Gives my heart a rush
If these walls could talk
They would tell the story
Of how I feel for you
And how I wish you felt for me
When you u speak I hang on your every word
(Though my friends may find this quite absurd)
I dream dreams of sharing my secrets with you
I wish and I pray for that day to come true
If these walls could talk
They would tell you the feelings I feel
And how a simple touch from you
Would make my broken heart heal

*Inspired by *HIM**

"Man of My Dreams"
Written in 2005

I awaken in the morning and see his face
His name is on my lips
Thinking of him starts my day
He is on my mind
No matter what I do
No matter where I go
No one compares to him
He is all I want in a man
He is all that I dream of

As I go through my day his name is on my mind
His face, his smile, his voice
I imagine him sitting next to me
He is on my mind
No matter what I do
No matter where I go
No one compares to him
He is all I want in a man
He is all that I dream of

I return home after my day, his smile is on my mind
Something he may have said or done brings a smile to my
face
The phone rings, I wonder if it may be him
He is on my mind
No matter what I do
No matter where I go
No one compares to him

He is all I want in a man
He is all that I dream of

What I wouldn't give to have him next to me
Just to talk to him
Just to be in his presence
Just to touch his hand
Just to hear his voice
Just for one sweet kiss
I pray for a chance to make it real

He is on my mind
No matter what I do
No matter where I go
No one compares to him
He is all I want in a man
He is all that I dream of

"My Everything"
Written in 2005

They see a crush
What I feel is beyond description
This is love beyond
Anything I've ever felt
When he smiles I smile
When he's sad my heart is heavy
I'm his other half
And he doesn't even know it
He holds my heart in his hands
And he doesn't even know it
He is the sun and I am the earth
How do I let him know
That he is my everything?

"My Secret Wish"
Written 11/2002

I wish I could hold you but you're so far away
If I had a chance to be with you I'd beg you to stay
It's not just your looks or your sex appeal
But these feelings inside are so strong, and so real
From the first time I saw you I had a crush
I never knew I could love someone this much
I wish I could tell you the secrets I keep
And you could trust me completely you have a friend in me
When I see you I know there's more than meets the eye
Each day it's harder for me tot keep my feelings inside
Your smile makes my day and it's amazing how much
I dream of being close to you, just one simple touch
I wish I could fly and rush to your side
But for now I must hold these feelings inside
You are everything I dream of, I wish you knew
How deep my feelings are for you
But in the meantime I'll keep you in my heart
And in my dreams we are never apart
I wish I could tell you but for now I keep
This secret in my heart of what you mean to me

Dedicated to "D"

"If Only You Knew"
Written October 2005

I don't remember what it was
That made you catch my eye
But when I see you
I feel connected to you
Is it that smile?
Is it your voice?
Is it your style?
Whatever it is, you're a part of me
And you don't even know it

Did you know that you're in my thoughts
Every day?
Did you know that you're in my prayers
Every night?
Did you know that you're in my dreams
Almost every night?

I know that people look at me and judge
But they don't understand what I feel
I know we can never be together
And that's fine with me
But did you know that I would be your best friend?

If you told me your secrets
They would stay with me in my heart
You could share your joy with me
You could even share your pain
And I'd never let you down

Because you mean so much to me
I would be your homie, your friend
The one you can count on thru thick and thin
And when you do find that special someone
I'd be the one you can count on
If you ever needed a female's POV
I wouldn't hate, I'd congratulate
Because you mean that much to me

I know I'm pouring out my heart
And you don't even know me
You've only met me once
And that one time I still treasure
And hope that maybe we will meet again
And you will be my friend

If only you knew
How much you mean to me
If only you knew
How much I want to be your friend

"I'm Sorry"
Written 9/14/2006

If I ever made you feel smothered
Or less than loved and cherished
If I ever made you feel that you were not
The man for me
If I ever said anything to hurt you
Or piss you off
If anything I've done or didn't do made you feel that
You were not number one in my heart
I'm sorry

If I trip out on you, or forget that this is as much a struggle for you as it is for
me
If my words cut, when they shouldn't
If I never said it before, I'm saying it now
I'm sorry

Dedicated to Rocco

"I'm Yours"
Written 9/14/2006

I'll be here to hold you, be the lady by your side
Through thick and thin, your ride or die chick
I'm the one that loved you from the very start
I gave you my heart, what will you do with it
Will you cherish it?
Will you break it?
For you I'll be there always
To love and cherish
I'm yours till the very end
Your homie, your lover, your friend

God's Love

The pieces of my life began to come together when I gave my life to God. Not just in the "I believe in a higher power" way, but completely surrendering my life to Him. By allowing Him to take complete control, and understanding that He is the head of my life and not just someone to run to when things go wrong, I've learned to see life in a whole new light.

The chains of depression and not being able to love myself have been broken because I see myself as I truly am – a beautiful, new creation in Christ. I'm not here to preach religion, but to share my experiences. I hope and pray that by sharing my experiences, someone else out there will be blessed.

This section is inspired by my Lord and Savior Jesus Christ, and is dedicated to my late Grandmother Dorothy E. Queen and my late Great Grandmother Mollie T. Moyler who taught me how to pray. Thank you. Those lessons truly saved my life.

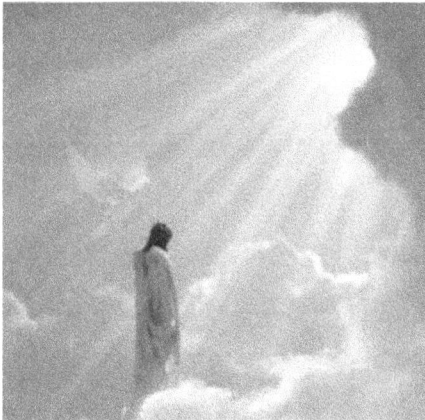

"A Smile"

A smile can attract, cheer up those around you. It can express a feeling of joy inside. It can be coy or bright, a subtle gesture or a hearty laugh. But that's not always the case...

Sometimes a smile, coy or bright, can be a disguise to cover pain. Fear. Sorrow. Anger. A storm of emotion roars inside. But others do not see...

A smile gives the illusion of happiness, but in darkness tears prevail. A smile gives the illusion of contentment, but fear prevails inside. I sit and wonder when it will end, then I stop wondering and crying and I take control...

I stop reaching for the answers from those around me, and I reach for a higher power to guide me. I stop sinking into self-pity, and I start finding myself. I start to break out of my shell, and I spread my wings. And how did I begin my journey? With a smile.

"My Prayer"

Humbly, Father, I come to You
I cast away my cares
I've been through tests and trials
I thank You for the tests
Because without them I have no testimony
Thank You for being my rock, my salvation
Thank You, Lord, for your saving grace
Though I don't deserve it
Your grace is a gift I do not wish to take for granted

Help me to become the woman
That You would have me to be, Lord God
Replace my tears of suffering with tears of joy
Replace the emptiness inside
With Your joy and peace
Let Your Light shine through me
And help lead others to You
Heavenly Father, help me to be patient
Help me to be forgiving
Help me to approach each situation in my life
With the question, "What would Jesus do?"
And help order my steps in Your word
As I go upon this journey
This I pray in the precious name
Of Your Son, Jesus Christ
Amen

"Wonderfully Made'
8/2/2007

I used to ask God why
I couldn't be pretty like the models in magazines
Why my hair wasn't long, why my skin wasn't perfect
Why my hips were so wide
Why my lips weren't pouty
Why my eyes weren't hazel like my sister's or blue like my Great Great Grandma's
Why other girls could eat and not gain a pound
But I look at ice cream and gain five
Why I couldn't turn boys' heads
Why I couldn't be slim
Why I couldn't be like "them"... whoever "they" are

Then God opened my eyes and my heart
"I am an Artist, and every member of the human race is a masterpiece
Created by My hands, just the way I planned."

Then I realized that I am beautiful

I am a new creation in Christ
God knows every hair on my head and doesn't care if I'm having a bad hair day.
My lips may not be pouty, but they speak the truth and sing beautiful songs.
My eyes may not be hazel or blue, but they see beauty in the world.
My body may not be slim, but it is beautiful because for nine months it carried a child
So wonderful, and such a gift.
So I no longer define myself according to "them"... whoever "they" are
I am God's work of art, wonderfully made.
A light in the world, a living testimony of His Goodness.

"Words from My Father"
5/2/2007

Fear not my child for I am here
When you cry it is I who dries your tears
When you screamed in the night it was I who eased your fears
And in My presence your depression disappears

I've taken your sadness, replaced it with My song
When you were weak, it was I who made you strong
The world called you defeated, said you were hopeless
You are Mine, My work in progress

The world could not see My plan for you
They could not see that I'm molding you
The world wonders how you keep a smile on your face
It is because in the midst of your trials you knew My grace

Fear not the words and plot of the enemy
Because you believe I have set you free
Cast away your doubts, leave behind your fears
Do not shed another tear

You may not see the light yet but fear not I am here
The demon of depression is cast out, do not fear
I did not forsake you through your tests and trials
I've been holding you up every inch, every mile

Your tears, your prayers were not in vain
For at the dawn of this new day, you're praising My name
The loss that you felt was not a true loss you see
I removed obstacles and barriers so that you can see

Your path is now clear, follow Me and take My hand
The world cannot open doors for you the way I can
The world labeled you "baby mama", a statistic in life
I label you "Mother" and one day "Wife"

As I change you on the inside, remove negativity
Your eyes are now open to possibilities
The world labeled you, but those labels are cast out
Throw them into the fire with depression and doubt

I've been your Comforter when no one understood
I've been your Best Friend when no one else could
I sustained you through trials when you lost your way
When "friends" disappeared I was glad to stay

Lean not unto your own understanding, I am He
The One who will supply your every need
I'm your Doctor through sickness, your Keeper in health
Every bill has been paid with no material wealth

You are not society's outcast, or a fallen victim, oh no
You are a Child of God - this the world will know
You are healed from depression; you are healed from your broken heart
Step into the Light; do not hide in the dark

Your life is a testimony, don't be afraid to praise
Because I lifted you up - celebrate all that is raised
I brought you angels to show you what you can do
And now you have a testimony in your own life too

Cast away the labels, the chains society gave
You are a Child of God - your life reflects My Name
The enemy is defeated; he can no longer hold you down
Smile my child - a new season is here, blessings abound

"Someone Prayed for Me"
Written 3/27/07

When I was at the end of my rope
When I thought I couldn't take another step
When I thought that all was lost
Someone prayed for me
I couldn't see light anymore
Thought all hope was gone
When I was sure I couldn't hold on
When I thought everything was going wrong
His light shone on me
And He set me free
And I know it's all because
Even when I couldn't find the words to pray for myself
Someone prayed for me

Dedicated to my Grandma. Your prayers pulled me through
more than anyone will ever know.

"Invisible" – The Story

I recently wrote a story based on my poem "Invisible". The story is told from the point-of-view of the main character, Kandi. She's a good girl who has dreams but is slightly blinded by her infatuation with Kevin Brown, the 2nd in command of Atlanta, GA's most notorious drug gang. She dreams of becoming his number one and helping to save him from his life of drugs, guns, and constant life-or-death choices. He's wrapped up in the game, and his girlfriend Jalissa. Here's a preview:

```
Chapter 1:  The Beginning

     This was the tightest clique in town... Derek and his brothers
Kevin, Pierre, Carlos and Brian ran the city.  They had money stacked
to the ceiling but they were slick enough to avoid the police.  They
did a lil bit of everything... Derek was introduced to the drug game at
a young age and by the time he was 13 he had a growing empire.  He
brought his brothers into the game, even his youngest Brian was brought
in as a lookout when he turned 11.  It was the only life he had known
and it brought in more cash than most people had seen in a lifetime.
Since they were the richest guys in town they were also the most sought
after by all the girls.  Their boys Chris, Rashad, Roc, Trey,  and Drew
were part of the operation.  Their boy L.J. wasn't slangin, he was
tryin to come up in the music game.  But he had been best friends with
Chris since they were little so he was cool with the Brown boys and
their crew.

     Derek met my cousin Alicia when they were still in middle school.
He liked her immediately, but he had to grow on her.  She thought he
was trying way too hard and finally in 10th grade she gave him a chance
and they've been inseparable ever since.  Jalissa fell for Kevin the
day she first saw him.  Her family had just moved from Miami to ATL and
Kevin came outside to mow the lawn.  He only mowed one section cuz he
wanted to keep his eyes on her.  And she couldn't take her eyes off
him.  They exchanged numbers and they've been inseparable ever since.
Pierre and Renee were best friends from kindergarten so it wasn't much
of a surprise when they started going out.  Nikki and Carlos used to
fight constantly since the day he put blue in her hair when they were
in pre-kindergarten.  Somewhere around 8th grade they discovered that
they actually liked each other.  DiAndrea and Brian were each other's
first girlfriend/boyfriend.  Both of them were too grown for their own
good at times but they were like a young Bonnie and Clyde.  Chris and
Coco had been going out since 9th grade.  Same with Joy and Rashad.

     The Brown boys' cousins Elissa and Evette were always with the
crew.  Evette was going out with Roc, who was kind of shy but knew how
to make money and how to treat a lady.  Elissa was dating Roc's homeboy
Trey.  My cousin Jan had been bunned up with our boy Drew.  We called
her "Twin" because she has an identical twin named Jerri.  Jerri moved
to Philly as soon as we turned 18.  And me?  I'm Kandi.  And L.J. is my
best friend.  We met back when my cousins and I first moved to ATL from
DC back when we were little.  Everybody thinks we should be going out,
```

but he's more like a brother to me. There is someone who is very
special to me... but he doesn't know it.

Summer 2004
Atlanta, GA

    We were all chillin at the Brown boys' house. Kevin, Derek and
Pierre were counting money... more money than I had ever seen in one
place at one time. I was sitting with L.J., Chris and Coco watchin TV.
Brian was sitting by the door with DiAndrea on his lap. Kevin opened
up the conversation. "Aye Kandi, you singin at the club Friday night?"

    "Yea.   You comin?" I answered, trying not to sound too anxious.
"I might come thru," he said half-heartedly. "I ain't got my party on
in a minute." L.J. interrupted, "You know Jalissa don't want you up in
no club."

    "Jalissa don't control me!" Kevin fired back.   Laughing, Derek
disagreed, "Dude, she got you whipped! She says jump and you say how
high, stop fakin!"

    "You betta shut up and count dat money!" Kevin snapped, his
feelings obviously hurt. "You know you gon drop about a grand on hair
gel." Pierre, who was usually the jokester of the fam yelled out,
"Hair gel!! hahaha Kevin got you dawg!" Kevin was on a roll, so he
continued, "And speakin of hair, you need yours cut!"

    "Renee likes my fro!" Pierre protested. "Says who?" L.J.
laughed. Pierre was unfazed as he fired back, "Whatever man! L.J.,
when you gon join us and make some of this money?"

    L.J. shook his head. "My music is gonna make me some money."
Derek laughed, "Dude, no disrespect, but you've been writin songs since
you were 10 and you still pushin a 1980 Dodge Omni!" L.J. stood his
ground. "But my Lula belle gets me everywhere I want 2 go." Pierre
laughed, "Your Lula belle is effin 24 years old!"

    "She's a classic!" I tried to put some points in L.J.'s court.
But Kevin bragged, "I'm pushin a Mustang convertible! My baby is
sweet!"

    Derek's mind was back on business. He commanded, "Open the
vault, Chris."

    Chris whined, "Why I gotta open it? I'm ova here chillin wit my
boo!" Kevin advised, "If you want your cut I suggest you do what the
man says." As he got up from the sofa, Chris announced, "Opening the
safe!"

    Jalissa, Alicia, and Renee came to the door and Brian yelled,
"Yall better announce yourselves."

    Jalissa gave him attitude, and shot back, "You betta let us in
half-pint!" "I know!" Renee cosigned, then playfully hit him. "Actin
like you don't know who we are!" Brian tried to look and sound
innocent as he spoke. "Aye, I'm just doin my job!"

I glanced over at the table. Kevin was poetry in motion...
everything about him was perfect. His smile, his eyes, his lips, the
way he moved, the way he spoke. But what was I thinking? He would
never check for me. He was so into Jalissa and I was lucky if he had
2 words for me when we hung out together. Jalissa sat on his lap and I
felt a pang of jealousy.... it hit me like a kick in the gut. I tried
not to look their way when they were together. He hugged and kissed
her and gave her all the attention I dreamed that one day he'd give me.
I felt a tear come to my eye when he whispered in her ear and she
giggled. But I held it back and painted a smile on my face.

Roc's Escalade pulled up, and he got out with Evette, Trey, and
Elissa. They came to the door.... Brian yelled, "Announce yourself,
fool!!" "You betta move it Half-pint," Roc barked as he entered. "I
mean seriously," Evette laughed, "Do we have to go through this every
time we come over here?" Again, Brian justified, "Just doin my job!"
"Well here's another job for ya," Evette started, "Go get me a soda.
Sprite, with a lemon wedge on the side. Easy ice. Make it snappy."
She snapped her fingers, then sat down next to Roc. Brian quickly went
upstairs to get the soda.

After the money was counted, and locked away in the safe, Derek
asked the room, "So what are yall tryinna get into tonight?" Kevin
quickly answered, "I say we hit up Flava."

"Flava?" Alicia scoffed. "We went there last weekend. Why don't
we hit up Eleven 50?" Jalissa protested, "Girl ain't nobody tryinna
hear that! I vote for Flava." Derek interrupted, "Hold on now, let's
take a vote. My baby likes Eleven 50, Kev and Jalissa vote for Flava.
Any other suggestions?"

Brian came back downstairs with a glass of Sprite in his hand,
with a little ice and a lemon wedge on the side just as requested. As
he got to the bottom of the stairs, he suggested Gameworks. DiAndrea
agreed, "I'm with my boo."

I made a suggestion, "I vote for Halo." Elissa asked, "Where's
Halo?"

"It's right on West Peachtree," I explained. The music is hot,
it stays open mad late, and I know the DJ and two of the bouncers.
FREE VIP DAWG!!" Surprisingly enough, Kevin agreed, "Sounds like a
plan to me!" Jalissa whined, "But baby, I really wanted to go to
Flava!" She started pouting.

Renee interceded, "Aww, girl suck it up we're goin VIP for free!"

Evette asked, "Well, what are we standin around for? We need to
get freshed out and get it movin!"

Pierre was excited, "Halo it is!"

Brian asked, "Can me and Di come too?"

"Of course... just like always!" I answered. "Just keep ya lil
young butt away from the bar unless you're drinkin apple juice." I
laughed so hard.

"Man, you must be the only 10-year-old that's been to almost every club in ATL!" Carlos observed.

"Hey, I'm 10 and 9 months!" Brian pointed out. "And I got it like that!"

Derek explained, "It comes with the territory. It's an advantage of bein the lil brother of DEREK THA DON!"

I called my boy to let him know we were comin through and it was all good. Jalissa cut her eyes at me... I wondered for a moment if she knew that I was majorly crushin on her man. But she was my homegirl, I would never seriously make a play for him. Maybe I was just being paranoid... she was probably just a lil salty cuz she was outvoted.

We all went home to get ready for the night. Then we rolled out.... L.J. wasn't allowed to drive Lula belle when he was with us so we rode with Derek and Alicia in his Lexus LS430. Kevin and Jalissa followed in his Mustang. Roc, Evette, Trey and Elissa rolled out in Trey's Mercedes truck. Pierre wasn't old enough to have his license yet, but he was pushin a 2005 drop top BMW. Renee rode shotgun, Brian and DiAndrea were in the back. The rest of the crew rode with Chris... who wasn't old enough to have a license yet either but was pushin a pimped out Suburban.

We hit the club and there was a line wrapped around the corner. Everyone was looking at us with envy as we walked right up to the door and got in with no problem and went straight to VIP. We looked and felt just like superstars, and always were treated as such. Forget buyin a drink, we were buyin the bar. Whatever we did, we did it to the limit and then some.

Nina Sky's "Move Your Body" came on and all us girls hit the floor givin the boys somethin to look at. We loved bein us - every guy wanted us but we were already with the city's top ballers, plus we were makin our own dollars. Some dude tried to approach Elissa - obviously he was new in town and didn't realize who she was with.

"Aye Pretty Eyes, what a nigga gotta do to get the digits?"

Elissa sized him up and answered, "Thanks for the compliment, but I don't think you wanna do that. My man is pretty jealous."

"Maybe you need a new man."

"Naw, I'm pretty happy with the one I have. You ever heard of Young Millionaires Crew?"

"You roll wit dem??"

Trey coolly walked up to them and put his arm around Elissa. "Yea she do." He flashed the hammer and the man took a step back. "I don't think we want no problems here," Trey continued, pointing to his piece.

"No disrespect man, I didn't know," the man took another step back.

"Well now you know," Trey said in a cocky tone.

"Lean Back" dropped and all the fellaz hit the floor.

Jalissa bragged, "Look at my man, he just know he too sexy. And that girl in the blue betta back the f*ck up 'fore she get rolled on."

Alicia laughed, "Dang, Jalissa, calm down."

"Uh-uh girl, I will wreck a bitch for my man. We been through too much and if ANY bitch think she can step in and take him she will feel the wrath."

"He would so be worth fighting for," I thought to myself. But I didn't dare say it out loud. I kept glancing at Kev, I couldn't help it. My heart raced whenever I saw him, heard his name or even thought about him. But I tried to fight off the feelings. Jalissa was my homegirl but I had to admit I envied her. Kevin had my heart and didn't even know it. Then Kevin Lyttle's "Turn Me On" came on. We all got in a huddle, coupled off and danced. We were all havin fun, switchin dance partners. Near the end of the song I was dancing with Kev.

"You think you can handle me?" I asked playfully as I began to wind my waist.

Kevin smiled, "Girl, see if you can keep up with me!"

I got lost in the moment... I let the music take me and I started winding and grinding, showing off, and I pulled him close to me. He didn't protest and I smiled. I could tell he liked the way I was workin it on him. He put his hands on my waist and moved with me. Through the corner of my eye, I noticed Jalissa was dancing with Rashad. She glanced at Kevin and me and immediately left Rashad and approached us.

"Excuse me Miss Kandi, gettin a little close aren't you?"

Kevin smiled, "Awww, my baby gettin jealous?"

I tried to stay calm. "No disrespect, J, we're just havin fun."

"Too much fun for me," Jalissa snapped. "Kev, can you come with me to the bar. I'm feelin a little thirsty."

"Ight, J."

My heart sank into my stomach.... he didn't even look at me again. He was focused on her and once again I was Miss Invisible. I wanted to cry but I refused. I just started dancing again until the DJ threw on a slow song. All the couples danced except Kevin and Jalissa who were at the bar whispering in each others' ears and sharing sweet moments that I wish he was sharing with me. L.J. was dancing with some girl that had been eyeing him since we walked in. Guys started asking

me to dance but I turned them down.... none of them were Kevin. I just
sat at the other end of the bar and tried to ignore them while I
drowned my sorrows in a strawberry Bacardi Silver.

    We closed down the club and as I walked out to the parking garage
my heart broke into pieces when I saw Kevin and Jalissa leaning against
his Mustang kissing like newlyweds.

    Derek snapped, "Get a room!" Alicia agreed, "Yea, we don't need
to see all that!" Kevin blushed, "Sorry yall, I can't help it. My
baby got me under her spell."

    "And you've got me under yours," I thought to myself as I
watched him. Even with traces of Jalissa's MAC lip gloss on his lips
he still looked sexier than the law should allow. I couldn't wait to
get home and get some sleep. The Bacardi was going to my head and I
was feeling woozy.

    Coco yelled, "AFTERPARTY AT KANDI'S CRIB!"

    All I could manage to say was, "Huh?"

    Chris continued as if he didn't hear me, "Yea! No parents, no
rules! Let's go!"

    I yelled in protest, "Did Kandi agree to this?"

    Derek smiled, "Don't be a party pooper, Couz!" Evette cosigned,
"Yea, I still wanna shake a tail feather!"

    Kevin and Jalissa were in another lip lock. I finally agreed,
"Fine, but somebody hose down the newlyweds over there!" Jalissa
laughed, "Don't be mad cuz you and L.J. won't go head and hook that
up!" I had to calm my temper.... She didn't know what was really up
with me and L.J.. I loved him but I loved him like a brother. I
couldn't picture myself with him on any other level. But I didn't want
any drama so I held my comments in and we rolled to my house.

    We had some drinks, listened to some music, watched some DVD's.
We were havin fun, and all the couples were bunned up. Kevin and
Jalissa went upstairs first, then Derek and Alicia were about to go
upstairs. I joked, "I'mma charge yall for those rooms if anything
jumps off!" Derek played along, "I'm good for it!"

    "I'mma charge $309 plus tax just like the Atlanta Marriott
    Marquis!"

    Derek laughed, "Girl I got about a couple grand on me right now
plus the safe back home looks like the cash cow at a bank!"

    I smiled back, "I don't want your money homie. Just don't go
messin up my sheets."

    I was joking but if I wanted to I could have made my crib a bed &
breakfast. I had 10 bedrooms, all decorated with different themes.
The master bedroom was mine, my mom had the smallest room. She wanted

it that way cuz she was hardly ever there. I had pretty much been taking care of myself since I was 11.

We looked up and realized Brian and DiAndrea had gone off somewhere.

Evette laughed, "Uh-uh, where did the youngins go?" Roc speculated, "Probly playin doctor in the den." I was shocked, and I shot back, "Shut up ya NASTY!"

I ended up dozing off on the couch next to L.J. As the sun was coming up over ATL, I heard Jalissa giggling as she walked down the stairs with Kevin. I knew that giggle... that was a "morning after" giggle. All I know is they betta had changed the sheets and made up the dayum bed!

Friday rolled around and I was chillin with my gurls. The guys had to drive down to East Point to take care of some "business".

"I know Kevin betta call me," Jalissa thought out loud. "They'll call when they're on their way back," Alicia reassured her. I worried out loud, "Don't you worry about the guys when they gotta make these deals?"

"Yea," Renee answered, "But they know what they're doing, they won't get caught." Alicia elaborated, "Even if they do, Derek got most of the Atlanta P.D. in his pocket. They'll get a slap on the wrist then hit the streets again before sunrise."

"Yup!" Renee cosigned. Then Jalissa changed the subject and asked me where L.J. was.

"Rehearsing for this show he's doin at Flava tomorrow night," I answered. "You need to go head and hook that up. Whatcha waitin for?" Her words really irritated me, but I laughed, "L.J. is hella cool but I don't see him that way. He's my boy." Before I could comfortably change the subject, Jan interjected, "I hate to be the one to break it to you Couz, but you need some lovin in your life."

"Yes, Kandi. You need a boo!" Alicia agreed.

Then Evette jumped on the bandwagon, "Roc's boy Black is single. And I heard he's checkin for you."

"Thank you all but I'm perfectly happy," I lied.

"Stop frontin," Elissa laughed. "I read all those love poems you wrote. You want a boo!"

I grit my teeth and shot back, "I am a strong, independent woman. I make my own money, push my own whip, pretty soon I'm gonna own my own house. I'm fine all by myself."

"I hear you Miss Independent," Alicia started, "but can your money, your whip, or your future house hold you and keep you warm at night?"

"My blankets keep me nice and toasty," I snapped back sarcastically.

"Girl, Kevin is my blanket!" Jalissa laughed. Coco joined in, "I know that's right, girl!!"

"Yall are nasty!!" I was really disgusted, imagining Kevin touching Jalissa. Joy snapped back, "Don't hate cuz we gettin our groove on! I think you should hook up wit L.J., he's feelin you girl."

By then I was really getting angry. "I told you, I don't need a boo. I'm good," I barked. Then Alicia jumped in, "Yea, and you're also celibate."

"SHUT UP!"

Alicia and the rest of the girls laughed.

"You know I'm just playin with you girl, lighten up," Alicia laughed and gave me a hug. Just then, Jalissa's cell phone rang. She took the call and a concerned look came over her face…..

If you enjoyed the preview of "Invisible", go to http://www.lulu.com/content/1098800 to order the book.

About the Author

J'Wan Yvette was born and raised in Prince George's County, Maryland. She was raised by her maternal grandparents, and graduated from Fairmont Heights High School. She attended Prince George's Community College where she studied Television, Radio and Film. Writing and music have been her passion since she was a child.

She began singing at the age of 3, and writing poetry and songs at the age of 5. She sang in her elementary school chorus, and as a teenager she sang with her church choir at Abyssinia Baptist Church in Maryland. She began writing short stories and plays at the age of 13.

J'Wan is also a single mother of a daughter, Jessica, who was born in February 2000. Having her daughter breathed new life into J'Wan. She had given up music and writing around 1998, but rediscovered her gift and found new inspiration when she became a mother. Now she aspires to publish her short stories and poems, and plans to bring her plays to the stage, and possibly the silver screen.

J'Wan published her first poetry book, ***Words of Love and Life: an Emotional Journey*** in 2007. She is currently working on more short stories, plays, and poetry. On a musical front, her single *"What Could It Be"* is available for download at http://stores.lulu.com/KandiGyrl808. She is in the recording studio working on new songs for an R&B/Soul which will be released in 2009.

Contact J'Wan at jwan@jymstonemusic.com or www.myspace.com/jwan808

This work is dedicated to Jessica, Gram, and my Muse

www.ingramcontent.com/pod-product-compliance
Lightning Source LLC
Chambersburg PA
CBHW030958090426
42737CB00007B/586